Power IN Words

A collection of poetry written by
HILARY BESSON

ISBN-10: 0-9985681-0-4
ISBN-13: 978-0-9985681-0-2

See more of Hilary Besson's art and creations at www.hilarybesson.com

All Rights Reserved © 2017 Hilary Besson. First Printing: Jan. 2017.
Published by HGB Publishing
No part of this publication may be reproduced, distributed, or transmitted in any form or by any means. No portion of this book may be copied, retransmitted, reposted, duplicated, replicated or otherwise used without the express written approval of the author.

Any unauthorized copying, reproduction, translation, or distribution of any kind of any part of this material without permission by the author is prohibited and against the law.

The cover art of this work was created by author, artist, and publisher Hilary Besson. Any replication of this work of any kind by any means is illegal.

All artwork and photographs showcased in this book belong to the creator, author, and publisher Hilary Besson. No part of any photograph or art in this publication can be copied, retransmitted, reposted, duplicated, replicated or otherwise used. Any replication, duplication, or copying of any kind by any means is forbidden and illegal.

Contact: hilarybesson@gmail.com

To my best friend and brother, Bradford Besson

Because I do not know where I would be without your endless support. Thank you for showing me courage and resilience every single day. You are the strongest person I know and you are special, never forget that. I love you to the moon and back.

* * *

Contents

This journey has no chapters.
This is a journey of truth and reality,
A journey that is not linear.
This is a journey whose order
Does not make perfect sense
Yet somehow makes perfect sense.
This is a complex journey
You are about to embark on because
This is a journey of love
This is a journey of kindness
This is a journey of self-worth
This is a journey of fortitude
This is a journey of justice
This a journey that is all interconnected
And this
This is a journey
That cannot be broken up
Into parts.

POWER IN WORDS

Introduction

Beautiful Scars: The Reason I Started Writing

This moment is so ingrained in my memory like somebody branded my amygdala with a heart; I was scarred but blemished in the most beautiful way possible. It's funny how experiences work like that. In the moment the pain is searing, but in the long run you're thankful for it. At first you wish you can rewind time to prevent it from ever occurring so you can remove the heartache you felt, but in the end you are always eternally grateful for its lack of evanescence because now, in some skewed way, you are beautiful for it.

I remember there was a fire in my stomach and a hurricane in my throat so ferocious it threw me through a loop. I had to double check my surroundings to make sure the words that came out of her mouth were truly spoken. It was too egregious for her to say, but it *happened* and I knew it. My mind spun, my head was clogged with a fog, and my heart felt as if it was being squeezed by a rubber band too small for its size. That atrocious feeling lingered with me for hours until I finally found my escape. My release was pen and paper, and my heart could breathe again. I will never forget the ferocity of my wrist as I scribbled my thoughts and feelings so intensely. I wanted to savor every reflection and slap it on paper before it ran away because sometimes thoughts have a tendency to escape you. But I could not let that happen, not this time.

I wrote and wrote until I felt better about the comment that hit me like a ton of bricks. It hit me hard enough to shock me but the force was not powerful enough for me to stumble, so I wrote and wrote and wrote until the swelling in my throat dulled. From that moment I discovered something: a thing so powerful it would change me without really changing me. I was not altered because I realized it had always been there, yet it changed me because I recognized it was unleashed. It was something so powerful that it could not have just arisen in that moment, it was merely hidden and I had not discovered it until then.

Now let me tell you something: there is nothing that hits you as hard as the race card. There is nothing so violent and disparaging. There is no analogy present on this very earth adequate enough to describe such a gibe with so much vigor. It's a feeling that I cannot truly explain in its entirety. If you've felt it, you would know what I am talking about. So that moment and the series of events that followed after the belligerence in her words fled from her mouth, was pivotal in my life. It was not the comment she made, or the audacity of her thought process, it was how I dealt with it. From that moment on I found a passion in writing and in words and in the ability to explain my well-being. More specifically, I found a passion for poetry, in the power to put my struggles and conquests on paper so I can cherish it forever.

This is not a small aspect of my being. This is not a minute hobby that I have come across. To the average person, who does not enjoy the art of literature, they will not even understand its level of importance but to me it has been paramount in finding myself. It has been paramount in the discovery of who I am and what I have become. So the average person may not understand its significance, but they do not have to.

So if I could, I would not rewind time to abolish the searing pain that struck my psyche because I am the sum of my experiences, wretched and painful, and that's not necessarily a bad thing. Consequently, I am thankful for the girl who tried to burst my bubble because she could not form one. I am disgusted by her prejudice but that is not the point. The point is I found beauty in a moment of ugly behavior. Although it pierced me and it left a scar, it was worth it. In fact, can you really consider it a scar or is it more of a beauty mark?

Now as you read through the collection of my poetry, I am giving you a slice of my world and a taste of all of my experiences. Remember that. And remember it all began with a beauty mark.

If it has the power to tear you down
It has the same strength to lift you up.

Words

Pen and Paper

I have a voice that needs to be heard
But nobody ever listens.
That's why I prefer
To talk to Paper
Because she's the only one
Who actually soaks up
What I have to say
In its entirety
And just
Listens.

I went 18 years without
Telling a single soul about my storms.

I went 18 years surviving
Hurricanes by myself.

There is a reason why there
Are so many books.
People want to tell their stories
When they have nowhere else to turn.

My First

The vacant page of
My first journal
Stared directly into
The depths of my soul.
It spoke with a tenderness
I'll never forget:
You can trust me for
I am a trashcan.
Litter me with the
Filthy secrets
You have been dying
To rid yourself of.

What if nobody gets it?
What if people don't understand my poetry?

Well
You don't write for them
You write for you.

Why, that feels so distant now
Like a dream
That is so encompassing,
So vivid and
Swamped with truth that
In the moment
It feels as though
Nothing else exists
Until you wake up and can
Hardly remember
What it is
You dreamt about.

Depression

Seven Hundred-Thirty Days

Two years is too long of a time
For a little girl to feel numb from the world.

I can't remember the last time I felt that way,
The last time the numbness consumed me
When my ears rang with white noise and
The air struggled to reach my lungs.
When it started with the lack of feeling in my toes
Turning into a numbness past pins and needles,
A numbness that became a parasite that
Consumed my entire being.

Sometimes though,
When times get really rough,
My toes still go numb.
But this time around
I don't let it consume me.

Drown yourself in your art, my love
Until your toes get that feeling back again

POWER IN WORDS | HILARY BESSON

She Shines and It Shows

My fingertips are sticky
With sugarplums and fairy dust,
Confetti spews out from my thumbs.
My mind is filled with streamers and
Glitter fuels my thoughts,
So I grab two pens and a paintbrush
Because oh! I must
Scribble and scribble
Until the voices are hushed.
Magic devours the pages
Whims are wired to my right hand
I converse in ink and acrylic because
That conveys each thought
Better than talking ever can.
Glued together by gum and silly string,
I pick apart each thought strand by strand
And the message is shot straight to my fingertips
Where they deliver it with their fixings,
Spectacular and grand.
My fingers stamp it on a
Canvas
Journal
Camera
Sketchbook
And many more alike

Because my brain is a disco ball
In the city that never sleeps.
It rages and splashes and dances
All night.

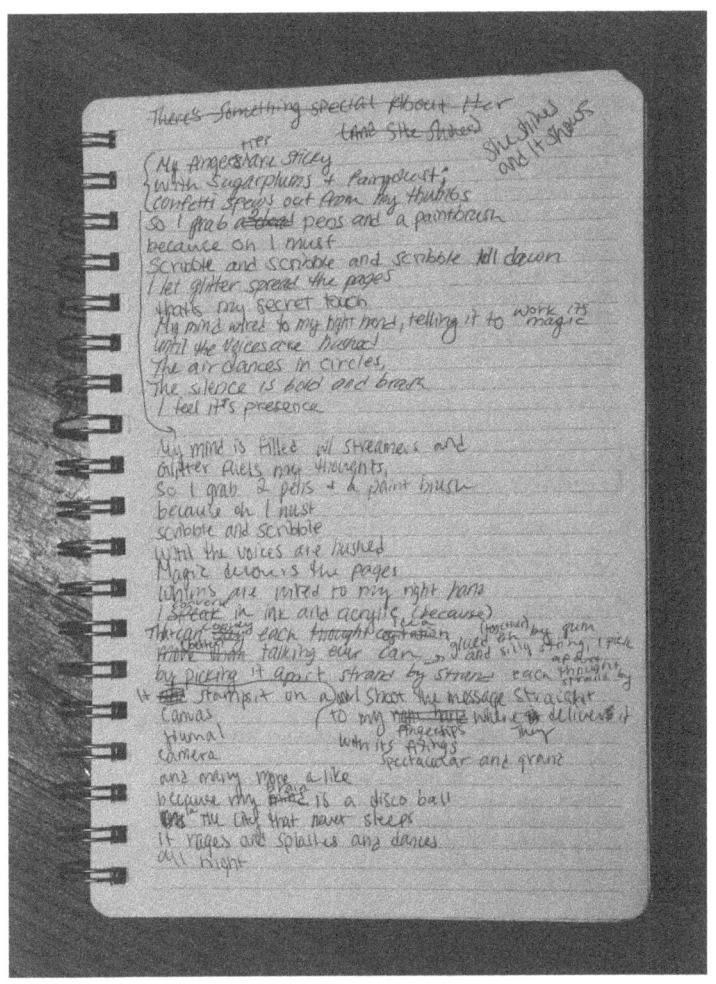

See look at that.
Look at you turning ashes into fairy dust.

I'm constantly told
I'm a ray of sunshine.

That's because
My flashlight was all out of batteries
And I needed something
To help me see through the darkness.

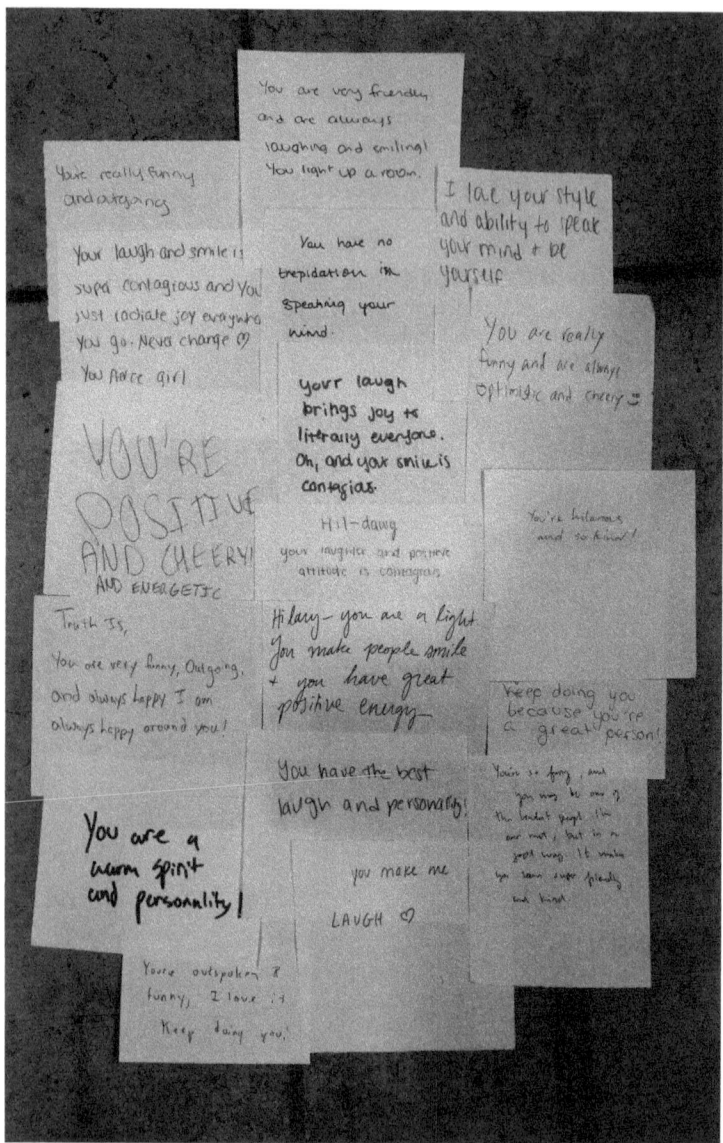

For a school activity, everybody in the class was told to write anonymous compliments to each other. These are a few that Besson received.

I'm known to set my world on fire
And I light up the room.
"How do you do it?" they ask
I say,
My blood carries
A tablespoon of butane.

I Am Light

Writing is my outlet
And when I allow myself to be
Plugged in to the most electrifying
Thing disguised in normality,
You would never it see it coming,
But lead scratches the
Surface of my journal and it
Sparks with such an intensity that
I could set this whole neighborhood to flames.

Watch out for that one.
She carries thunder in her back pocket.

It Doesn't Have to Be Christmas to Open Your Gift

You.
You, my friend.
You have a gift.
You smother it in bubble wrap and
Keep it locked behind closed doors
Because it's safe there.
No crooked mind can
Drown your dreams because
They don't even know it exists.
And it feels good that way
Oh it is pleasant
The gift that is solely yours
Wrapped in innocence before
A person sneezes on it,
Riddling it with germs
And water marks.

But something's not right.
You have your gift
Buried in cotton balls but
You don't really want to keep it there.
You want to open your gift in public but
You are frightened
Oh you are terrified

Because people have a tendency
To ruin beautiful things.
But that is only because
They haven't found their gift yet.
They are scavenging through waste
Or they have laid down
Before they've even started looking.
They're lost.
But, honey, that's not your problem.

It is not up to you
To hide your gift from the world
Because a select few may tarnish it.
No
It is up to you
To release your gift from
The prison you have kept it in
So you can bask in it
Along with the many who will celebrate you.

You.
You have a gift,
My friend.
For the world to see.
So you must take the leap and
Set it free.

Self-doubt
Is what crushes
Great dreams.

My Mama always asks me, "Baby, why are you so hard on yourself?" What I have always failed to explain is: I'm not hard on myself because I feel as though I am insufficient. In fact, it is quite the opposite. I'm hard on myself because I know exactly what I am capable of, so when I fall just one centimeter short of greatness I do not celebrate. I tell myself, *Yes you did well. But next time you will blow them away.*

My role is not to convince the world what I can do. My role is to convince *me* what I can do. Once I can do that for myself, there is no need to discuss my endeavors because I know what I have in store. With that being said, I am fully convinced that I can move mountains. So I keep my dreams to myself and grind in silence.

You Can Be a Chick or You Can Be a Rooster, but You Cannot Be Both

But what separates
The chicks
From the roosters?
Well the chicks
They are cute,
Dainty and fragile.
Their fluff steals
The hearts of many;
Beloved by most,
Irritated by few,
But that's about it
What else does it do?
But the rooster,
The rooster, however,
Has more than just pretty feathers.
Beneath its exterior
Lies a soul with drive.
The rooster arises
At the crack of dawn
Every single morning
Yodeling until
Its boom box skips a track.
People awake along with its cry
And they are angry at its vocals

Echoing through their sheds,
But the rooster is ruthless in its quest
To conquer its personal grail.
So yes
People will bark at the crowing bird
Until their throats bleed,
But the rooster has a job to do.
So the rooster continues to sing on
At the crack of dawn
Because the rooster,
The rooster will stop for no one.

There are two parts to dreaming,
Some tend to forget the latter.
Part I is the dream in imagination
Part II is giving it a spine
But there are no fairy godmothers
Or genies in bottles so
Don't snap wishbones,
Hush birthday flames,
Or count on 11:11
Unless you're willing to work
For what you wish.

Part II

Tic Tic Tic

I work hard in the shadows
And you do not have a clue
But there is a whole slew of
Greatness brewing in the stew.
Now at this point
It behooves me to tell you,
I'm the bomb
In the corner of the room:
You may not hear me when I'm ticking
But you'll hear me when I boom.

The reason I don't talk about my goals
Is because there are too many people
Who pretend to care.

They'll sit in silence and
Wait for you to fall
Because they have never
Seen success
Within themselves.

What you don't understand is
Secretly hoping someone else doesn't succeed
To match the failure
You have succumbed to
Doesn't make you any less alone,
It makes you an asshole.

The World Is Full of Assholes

Ants and Giants

Why does the fact that I feel big
Make you feel so small?

Although I may be great,
I am not greater than.

Although I may be light,
I am not brighter than.

This could be a world full of giants
If only so many of us didn't
Feel like ants in comparison to others.

Beauty Takes Many Forms
Beauty Is Not a Possession

It truly pains me when
Humans pretend not to see
The excellence in others
Because they feel as though
It inevitably
Takes away the value
In themselves.

This girl moves mountains
And freezes rivers.
She makes the stars align just for her.

"Pshh, I could've done that," they puff.

Than why didn't you?

People Somehow Can't Celebrate Others

Valentine's Day

People often wonder why Valentine's Day
Is my favorite holiday
When I don't have a hand to hold.
I say, *because it's the one day where people*
Can finally focus on celebrating one another.
I may not receive a dozen roses
Or an assorted box of chocolates but
Love is in the air
And that's enough for me.

Then again,
What do I know
About love.

Wait
You mean to tell me
I'm supposed to feel something?
Because I haven't felt it yet
And I'm dying to.

Sparks

Sometimes I spread my legs
Before they can even crack me open
Because I crave human connection
But reject the thought of them touching me
In the rawest form possible.

Emotional Proximity

We Used Each Other...

He used my body for sex
And I suppose I used him too,
But he came and went
Faster than a tornado spins
And my world was empty
For a short moment.
Empty in a way that it wasn't
Before he came and went.

Ladies
Please remember
You are worth
So much more
Than pried legs
And proud men.

Through Pried and Proud, Know Your Worth

We are taught to shove
Tampons up our sleeves and
Pads in our boots because
God forbid we show the world
There is anything more to us
Than white smiles and
Floral sun dresses.

The Beauty in Blood

Generally, blood is not considered an inherently elegant quality under any basic standards. As women, when it is part of our biology to bleed, but also our role in society to be "inherently beautiful," that is when there is a clash. We do not converse about our menstrual cycles in a tone above a whisper because it is in our culture to please the world with our eternal grace. So we hide what makes us women because, subtly and unconsciously, we are taught that part of us is not beautiful.

I watched as a stranger approached a girl.
He called her pretty
And she *beamed*
As if she didn't already know
How beautiful she was on the inside.
As if all she relied on was her
Outward appearance to feel whole.
As if nobody else had told her
She was pretty in years
So she began to feel
The ugly crawl through her veins.
As if a man's perception,
A man she doesn't even know,
Was indicative of her esteem.
As if that "compliment" summed up her worth. . .

She Beamed for the Wrong Reasons

Mirrors

If you look at yourself in the mirror
And the very first thing you see
Is that your nose is a little crooked,
Your waist should be 2 more inches cinched,
Your skin isn't flawless,
And goddammit your lashes just aren't long enough
Than, darling, you're not fit for mirrors
Because mirrors are there to remind you
How incredible you are and
If you can't see your own beauty
Before your very eyes
Than who else will?

Mirrors

Look at yourself in the mirror.
If you see ugly
If you see weak
If you see worthless
Than you are your biggest battle.
If you see beauty
If you see strength
If you see greatness
Than you have already won.

Reflections

How others treat you
Is a direct reflection of
How much you love yourself
In the most brittle sense of the word.
If somebody plays you for a fool
And you repeatedly stay by their side
Than you are one
Because you don't see how deserving you are
And that is so foolish.

Playing with Fire

The flame is dancing,
Flickering in the wind.
It extends its invitation
While wrapped in a bow
And doused in sin.
The flame is dancing,
Glowing, vibrant and alive.
Refusing to be ignored it calls her name
So she follows its path and sneaks inside.
Doesn't she know it senses her fragile mind?

Footprint after footprint
Step after step
It takes her to its secret crypt.
Fire ball with a halo,
An aura she can't ignore.
Enticing with its light,
It's the angel of hope
Leading her to its door.

But she steps inside
And it locks her in.
She looks into its evil eyes
And it flashes her a grin.
Before she can think

It multiplies upon itself.
She opens her mouth
And she cries for help.
Heroes respond with silence and
She loses all hope of being saved.
The door was latched from the inside
In which she stood
But the attention she craved.

As she burns to her death,
With the pain of her
Skin peeling back
Comes a final roar.
Damn
She's such a lonely fool.
She should have unlocked door.

Tell me why
You expected me to
Bounce back to you
After you jabbed me. . .
You must've mistook me for a
Punching bag.

I'm Not Coming Back

There Is Nothing for You Down There

Stop searching for love at the bottoms of oceans
When you know you have no business
Being down there.
Stop searching for love in someone
Who will let your
Vision go dark
Eardrums implode
And lungs collapse
In the hopes you might feel
Soft sand at the bottom
Because I'm telling you
There are rocks and creatures and
Broken bottles down there
That are too rough for your sensitive feet,
But you already know that.
You may have been deceived by its beauty
And enticed by its mystery at first,
But when you go deeper and deeper and
You begin to notice it's getting
Darker and harder to breathe,
I promise you that you're not
In too deep to turn back around.
That is when you must find it
Within yourself to rise to the surface
Where the sun shines brighter

Or else you'll never make it out alive.
I just hope you make it back before
They steal all of the oxygen you
Had left in your lungs but spared
Just to meet them
At the bottom of the ocean.

7 Billion

There are seven billion people in this world, I say,
Please explain to me
Why you always go back
To the one that hurts you the most.
Because she's the only one that gets me...
We have the same sense of humor...
We like the same music...
So you're telling me
There is no one else on this big blue earth
That will laugh at mismatch socks,
Listen to jazz,
And treat you right?
Nope...
And if there isn't?
You have to understand
You are enough
You are enough.

The last thing you shall let yourself do
Is count on others to fill your void.
You must be whole on your own.

He Doesn't Own Your Joy

So she left you.
She packed up your old sweatshirts
And tattered bracelets,
Wrapped them in boxes with your name spelt wrong.
So she broke your soul in half,
Scratched your name out from the bark.
So he left you,
Erased your memories from the sand.
So he stomped on your brittle heart,
Snatched your radiance and
The laughs you shared.
So he said happiness wasn't you
So he was your everything
So she made you forget the sadness that
Coupled with rainy days and dark clouds
So she was your other half
So she completed you.
So what now?
I guess it's about time
You stop
Trying to tape the pieces back together
And you start trying
To live for yourself,
Saying *I* complete *me*
With him or without.

We All Have a Dream

He offers me the world,
His hands outstretched.
I utter softly,
I've got a dream to catch.

He suggests rainbows and daisies
Wouldn't that be fine?
I reply with a coolness,
Honey, that's your dream not mine.

He begs me not to leave
But I've got plans ahead.
Tired of waiting, I repeat,
I'll pursue my dream instead.

I strut away
With my head held high.
He chases after me
Because his dream died.

I don't fear I'll fall in the arms
Of someone who treats me wrong.
I am much too great for someone
To treat me like I am not,
And this world is much too large
For me to feel stuck in place.
But maybe I won't be able to
Hold on to the one
Who treats me right because
I was never taught how to.

Vice Versa

When I grow up
I wish that somebody
Will love me like
My mother loved my father
And I hope I have it in me
To repay him
Like my father never could.

When I grow up
I wish that somebody
Will love me like
My father loved my mother
And I hope I have it in me
To repay him
Like my mother never could.

The Reason Why They Couldn't

They put their trust in one another. They loved each other to escape the shattered homes they came from. But they were young and naive and they fell too hard, too quickly, and at the same time. That's the part that ruined them: the fact that they fell at the same time. When you trust fall into someone's arms, you need a partner with a base stronger than yours, but they were both too broken to have knees that wouldn't quiver beneath them in order to catch one another. They had too much hope that the bliss would lift them, that the clouds would catch their fall. Their faith betrayed them, though, as they cracked their heads and their hearts on the wooden floor. In the end, they blamed each other when there were no real arms present to drop into. To break the fall. To stop the hurt. They loved each other but they both needed to be caught. Too bad that's impossible to do when they're falling at the same exact time.

I know what love is
Because I have seen
What love is not.

Divorce

My parents don't love each other anymore.
They showed me that love is one way tickets
To silent nights.
That love is wilting flowers on countertops that
They were too lazy to trash.
That love is caution;
That love is tiptoeing on hot coals
And praying not to get burned.

My parents don't want each other anymore
And that should tear my heart in half
But honestly
I wish it had happened sooner.
It would have spared us
The broken nights
When the air reeked of conflict.

There Were a Few of Those Nights

Oh those nights?
You can't take those back.
The nights when your teardrops
Formed puddles and
Your mascara smeared
Across your pillowcase,
Creating the one watercolor piece
You will never find beautiful.
The nights where your heart fractured
And eardrums cracked
Along with Mama's vocal strings
That hit one octave too high.
Her throat broke that night
And yours did too as
Its parts scattered
The floor of your stomach,
Cutting your innards.
You lay in bed and
Block your ears but
It's too late.
You've already heard everything.

Or the night when you were little.
The night when he ran through the back door
Frantically asking where she is
Because you know she's in the bathtub
And you know this time she might break for good.

Dangerous Woman

There are demons crawling in her head,
Her brain is the sum of worms writhing in summer heat.
Shooing away helping hands, instead
She pours mud in her skull
And ties her wrists to her seat.
She drowns in her thoughts, nothing is said.
Struggling to set herself free,
She traps her mind and rips it to shreds.
In her cranium she plants seeds
For the crows to peck and gnaw
And come and go as they please.
Her eyes are filled with polluted oceans,
Her eyes are blind with dread
A drop of blood, the water billows with red
Her twisted thoughts spread
She squirms in bed;
She can't sleep when she feels that dead.

A bubble within her stomach rises
But it grows and grows becoming larger than she
So in one big huff she belches
An earth shattering scream.
She roars and she growls loud
Deep enough to rip her at the seams.
A caution sign is stamped to her forehead

Blatant enough for her family to see.
She is volatile but she is loved
To say the very least
But danger lies within the fact that
She fails to see what we see.

That is part of the heartbreak,
She can't control the demise of her sanity.
Even though her loved ones are at stake,
She's in denial and will never flee.
I reach out and get bitten
Every single time.
I know she doesn't mean to hurt
Because she does not realize
What she does when her mind
Is covered in slime.
She'll smash pans and crack glass
It's excessive and scary
But she'll never agree.
She'll let out one more reverberating scream
Then sob she will
And for acceptance she pleads.
But don't you see?
She lashes out.
I want to help her
But she's dangerous to me.

How can you expect her to save you
When she can't even save herself?

She is fire.
She has repeatedly provided me life and light
But she has burned me so many times.

Confusion in Motherhood

It's Not Her Fault

It's not her fault
It's not her fault
It's not her fault
It's not her fault
It's not her fault

"I am not crazy!"
No, of course you are not.

But you are not well.

There is a difference.

I place myself in a shoebox
I hum a little hymn
I hug my knees and rock
Until my world slows its spin.

Safe Place

I need to get away.
I need to escape to a place
Where there are cotton candy clouds
And a lack of humans in my space.
A destination where I can walk on water
And feel the current rocking the tide;
Where I can float just inches above the lake,
Having no thoughts and a clear state of mind.
For most people, in order to be joyous
They need somebody by their side
But not me, what do I need?
Merely the aquatic dome where I can get away and hide.
Here the sky is on fire and the stars burst into flames.
In this moment I can live forever
Because here is not the same.
Here is different, it's not like any other hive.
Here I can watch the waves in silence
And finally reside.

Or I'll travel to the mountains,
Reaching the very peak,
Where I'm high enough to fly with the birds
That lead with their beak.
I'll feel the breeze in my hair

As it passes right through me
Then I'll let the ether steal my words
Because it's the best kind of thief.
Now I can sit atop of the trees
Becoming so in tune I fail to speak
And in this moment
I am at peace.
I'll close my eyes and let my body
Become one with the wind
Where I'm high enough to forget
About all of those who have sinned.
This is where I need to be in order to get away,
To become whole with myself and truly feel at bay.

Next I'll journey to the river.
There I lay and listen intensely
To the water pushing past the stones.
To my house I'll never return
Because here feels more like home.
The rocks stand their ground,
Solid and stubborn,
While the water is in a hurry and on the run.
Maybe the stream, too, is trying to get away,
Making me the water and the rocks all in one.
Fleeing but planted,
Dashing but fixed,
Is what I've become
Synonymous to the workings of the stream.
This is a paradox that works together perfectly.

I am the water and the stones and the creek
And they too are me.
An understanding I can only receive
Here where I have escaped
And am truly free.

Pack Your Bags

They, too, abandoned their broken souls
Along with the dusty couch
Sizzling on the concrete outside.
It was hot that day
And so were their spirits,
Fiery with heartache and agitation.
They abandoned that couch
And their home
Along with everything in it
Because they're moving out
And moving on to better things.
So one last time they glance at
That dusty couch
Roasting in the hot summer sun.
It is stained and splattered
With anguish and midnight suffering
Along with their rusty souls they are
Leaving behind
In the shackles they once called home
Because they are sick and tired of fixing it
Sick and tired of the tool kits
Sick and tired of band aids hiding scars
Sick and tired of being sick and tired.
So one last time,

Before stepping out,
They look back at that house and
The walls that were painted with sweat and tears.
They are done moving furniture into a broken home
Needing too many renovations,
Done packing their psyche to the brim
With strain and anxiety.
So they gather their belongings
And cram their empty hearts into their suitcase
Because they are moving out
And moving on.

The Seasons Are Changing

It's the start of September
And it's time for new beginnings.
Warmth is among us and
I'm ready to drink sunlight
But now suddenly
The seasons are changing and
The sun is playing
Hide and go seek. I sing,
Come out come out
Wherever you are
But it has failed to return so
The air is now cold
Because the seasons are changing.
Part of the problem is
I have left all of my hats at home.

The seasons are changing and
It's snowing in October.
The sky is crying frozen tears and
The leaves are falling;
This happens every year.
If the branches can't even hold onto the leaves
Than tell me how I'm supposed to
Hold on to relationships.
Tell me how the message of

All beautiful, colorful things are meant to die
Is supposed to leave me hopeful?
If the two things that
Sprouted
Grew
And flourished
Together
Can be separated
And stripped bare within a month
Where do I latch on to hope? Because
The seasons are changing
And the trees are naked.

The seasons are changing and
November stinks of
Frigid air
Chapped lips and
Broken furnaces.
A month that is drenched with nights
Where you are one blanket short of warmth.
The seasons are changing
And my hands are becoming numb.
I'm afraid it's too much
For my fragile fingers.

*   *   *

Why yes the seasons are changing, love

And trust me when I tell you
The sun may have hidden
And the leaves may have fell
From their branches
But, darling,
The sun will come back out and
The foliage will grow back again;
They've just gone away for a while.
The seasons are changing and as for
The leaves and the branches?
Well, they're creating new lives
Separate from one another
Until it's time for the sun to reappear
And for them to rekindle the connection
They've already had
Because trust me
When June rolls around
It'll feel like
They have never even departed
Because the seasons are changing
And that's how seasons work.

The seasons are changing, dear
And the air will become frigid,
Lips will grow chapped,
And furnaces may break
But you have sparked connections
With so much warmth
That it can heat a village

And you make the degrees rise:
It's supposed to be 35
But somehow you have made it 67
So hear me when I tell you
The seasons are changing
And November has never felt so warm.

I have never stopped loving you.
I could <u>never</u> stop loving you.
I just needed some time away
To remember just how much
I love you.

Darling, she loves you
She really does.
Just because she can't love you
The way you need her to
Does not mean she loves you any less.

And Mama
Just because I have been hurt
Does not mean I won't go
To the ends of this very earth
To make you happy because
Mama that's all I want for you.
And I know you have done
The best you could
To do right by me
So Mama I forgive you
For everything.
I hope you have the heart
To forgive me as well.

With Love,
Your Daughter
<3

Dear Mama

I came to my mother nervous and crying. I said,
"Mama I need to tell you something
Mama I need you to know that my
Writing gets really personal
And it's not meant to hurt you Mama.
Mama, I love you and
I don't want you to feel attacked."

She spoke in the gentle way that mothers do,
"Trust me, baby
I wish I could redo a lot of things,
But your feelings are valid and
I don't want to cause you anymore pain.
You're writing a book.
This is a time of celebration so
Don't hold back.
There will be no backlash
I promise you that."

<3
Permission

Ain't Nothing Like My Mother's Love

I don't think there is a scale large enough to accurately measure the amount of unconditional support my mother has provided me. She has done so much, but just to name one: she was at
> Every.
>> Single.
>>> One.
>>>> Of my sports' games.

I knew I could always count on seeing her in the stands with a smile on her face wide enough to split her cheeks. If I ever glanced over to find her absent, why traffic must've gotten to her before she could get to me because we both knew she wouldn't miss it for the world.
And let me tell you,
There ain't nothing else like that.

Thank You, Dad

Thank you for being soft with me
When I was the blade that cut right through you.
Thank you for being my hand to hug
And my shoulder to cry on
When I was not easy to hold.
Thank you for being my teddy bear to squeeze
When the demons were eating me up at night.
I love you so much.
Thank you for loving me endlessly.

"Me and your father may not be together
But he will always be my best friend."

Love Is Not a Ghost

It's not that they don't love each other anymore
Because they do.
I've learned you can't
Just make love disappear.
It's just that sometimes
The future doesn't work out
As you planned it.
The past, though, is engraved in stone.
There is transition but
There is no vanishing of what once was.

Family

My heart aches in the best way
At the thought of them.
It is filled with so much love that
It just might burst.

The Bounce Back Kids

I suppose there are
Benefits to growing up
In a home that
Creaks and cries,
Yet treats and tries.
A home that is comprised
Of sticks and stones
And happy endings
Because now
We are no strangers to adversity.

In the process,
You have raised the tough
You have raised the wise
You have raised the strong
You have raised the buoyant.

He Is a Gladiator

I know you live in a space
Where there are
Voices in the ceiling and
Rats in the walls.
I know you meet with
The monsters under your bed
Every Tuesday and Thursday.
But I also know they are no match to
The durability in your spine because
You're fighting it through and
Shaking them off
For all you can do is
Battle the giants as they come and
Take it one day at a time.

For Calvin Besson

He Is Unlike the Rest

He is strong.
His arms are made of rocks and tissue
But
I'm not referring to that.
I'm talking about the diamond in his dome
And the brick in his heart.
An organ can't hold a mass that heavy
But he's different
So he carried it around everywhere.
The weight began to sink to his knees
And his knees proceeded to plunge toward the earth.
His soul hurt
But his mind twinkled
And he knew it
So he outshone the pain
And he dug deep
Because he's different.
So he crawled for miles
And his palms began to bleed from the gravel
Until he finally found it within him
To stumble to his feet.
But it wasn't over
Not even close.
An anchor was stapled to his thigh
And he was stuck in place for a short while.
Anybody else would have

Descended to the ocean's floor
But he's different
And he's beginning to see that
So he used the strength
Harbored in his mind.
He grimaced hard
And veins shot out from his neck
But he dragged that anchor
Along with him on his journey
Because he's got somewhere to be.
His heart is heavy,
His knees weak,
His mind tired,
But that
Will not
Deter him
Because he has something special:
It's the diamond in his dome.
He's going places
And he has a date with defeat
Because he's different.
So he continues to hobble and limp
With all of his parts,
Arduous and cumbersome.
Because he's different.
Because he's too strong not to.

For Bradford Besson

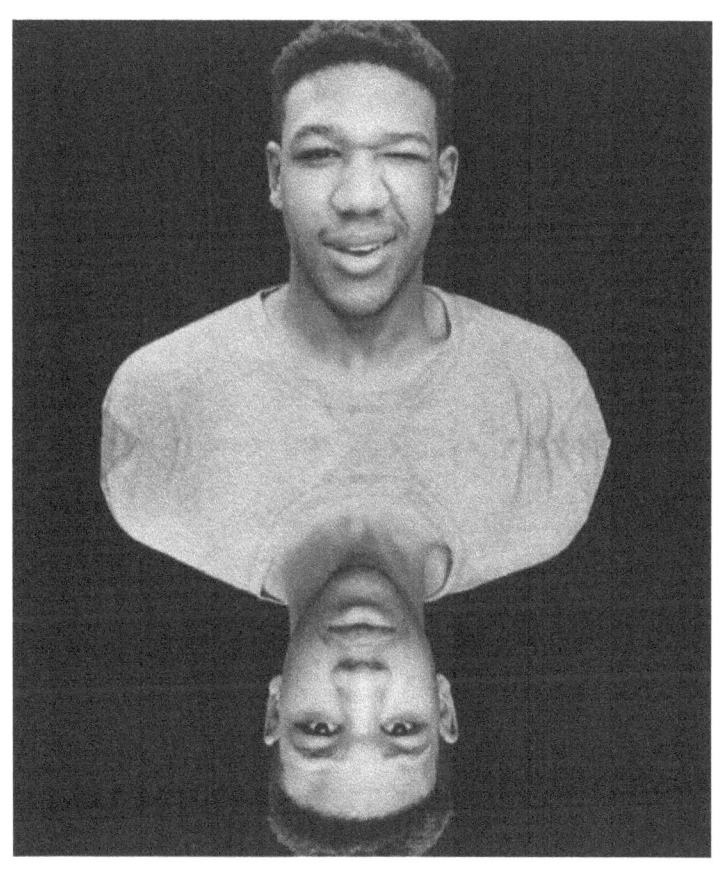

She Shoots for the Stars

She trudges through galaxies
With dinosaurs on her shoulders,
Her back straight like wilting flower stems.
The weight on her neck
Surmounts to pain far greater
Than the sun scorching her skin
So she drapes her cloak
Over her spine
To hide the pterodactyl
Stomping on her shoulder blades.
No one can see the pain
Radiating from her core
But maybe she can't either
For it is behind her.
Out of site
Out of mind.
Speaking of which
Her mind is the product of shards:
Sharp and steady,
So she keeps trudging on
Through the milky way.
She jumps from one star to the next
Whilst her feet are on fire with every leap
Until she lands on one fit for her.
Conquering it,
She stands on that star

Tall and mighty
As she allows her body
To be encompassed by flames.
The sparks on her shins
Match the ones in her retina.
The star:
It is hers
And she owns the galaxy.
But there's still a cramp in her neck.

For Myself

The Voice in My Head

Darling, you're not superhuman
Darling, you can only take so much
Darling, it's okay to break
It's okay to break sometimes, sweetheart.
Not even a diamond can hold
The weight of the world on its shoulders.
And look how far you've come,
Look how you're still standing
With the weight of the world stomping on you like that.
Look at me when I tell you, darling
Darling, that's more than a diamond could do.
And look at the way you sparkle
With this goddamn world
Chucking mud at you all the time.
I ain't ever even seen a diamond shine through the mud.
So yes, cry, darling
And let those tears form riverbanks
Because you can only take so much
Before your heart is bound to weep.
So keep on crying until you're all cried out
So you can stand tall again
And sparkle.

Here I Lay

Here I lay in my own abyss.
The silence is deafening
And I can taste the rise and fall of my lungs like
The moon's depart and
The sun's awakening.
There is chaos beneath its steady consistency.
As I peer through pitch black expanse,
I am fully encompassed,
Hugged,
By the darkness
But the warmth of its embrace
Cannot simmer the tremble in my being.
I breathe deeply
I breathe slowly
I breathe steadily
To bring the anarchy beneath the surface
To a screeching halt.
I am untangling my internal wires
To match my motionlessly structured outer shell
And I allow the silence to burst my eardrums
Until I am calm
Until I am ready
To be internally
Still.

Sometimes Life leaves me
With a knot in my chest
Too tight for my
Delicate fingers to unravel,
So I do not brawl with it.
Instead
I lay down,
Inhale deeply,
And wait for the pain to pass
To the point where
Even Life
Gets tired of pulling
A knot so tight
On someone
Who refuses
To squirm.

How are you so strong?
Because I had to be.
How do you mean?
Well
When abuse lives downstairs
You learn to grow gills
So you don't drown in the sorrow.

It's Instinct

When the Birds Sing

There are crippled birds out there
With broken wings and
Lost feathers.
There are crows
Who take their first flight
Twenty-one stories high
As well as vultures that
Gobble their young
And forget to die.
There are eagles with snapped beaks,
Ducks with no webs between their feet,
Owls who hug their own wings and
Shiver in the heat.
There are birds out there
Who don't migrate south
Because the pack journeyed without them
And they were left out.
There are crippled birds out there
With torn wings and
Dignity that stings
But
<u>Where the sky rises</u>
<u>The birds sing.</u>

The Little Flower That Could

There was a rectangle of concrete
With no life to be found
But add a little water,
You refuse to drown.
Instead you find life
And so it begins:
Weeds sprawl the surface
And you find the power within.
You push hard and propel upward,
The base begins to fissure and crack.
Your head breaks through the surface
And you refuse to look back.
From here you cannot be stopped,
Taller and taller you grow.
You have a peak to reach,
To all who said you couldn't you'll show.
Now you are flourishing
And leaves break out from your stem
Along with a few thorns;
This is your protection through chaos and mayhem.
Now your spine is tall and your stance is poised,
Petals bloomed gracefully from your stalk.
Look at you, you did the impossible
And sprouted from a cinder block.

Temporary

It comes and goes
You know
Like how the river flows,
Like the sand that seeps between your toes,
Like the fall of fresh petals on that rose.
There, too, are pros
To how life goes and goes
Like the whitehead on your nose,
The misery in your woes,
And the snow that froze.
So it shows:
It's in the wind that blows,
The dream that grows,
The feelings you chose
Because, you know,
Everything is temporary.
Everything is temporary.

You're Running Out of Time

I am a festering sore,
Who can't bear it anymore
So I crack the window and
Slam the door
Because I need air to breathe
And sanity to store.
The days are dying down
WHAT!
I only have four?
That can't be so
I swore I had more.
I'm extracting juice from clocks
And I make it
Pour
Pour
Pour
Down the depths of the drain
Until the pipes snore.
My muscles ache
Yet they're not quite sore
SHIT!
How much time is left?
I'm not sure anymore.

Living Watercolors

Life is moving too fast
For me to grasp
And everything is a blur.

Before You Die

There were skeletons and mirrors
And they were ready for some fun.
Smoke entered their lungs
And laughter escaped their throats
As they danced without the sun.
They always wait
For the moon to glow
And for the stars to kiss the black skies,
Because when all are asleep
And there's no one to weep
That is when they rise.
And so they frolic,
Their shriveled bones
Meet the shining glass.
With their reflection
The crystal reveals
Not only their dented skulls
But also their past.
Because every night
When the sun goes down
They always journey back.
They cheers to the olden days
When their bones were clothed
With fluids and flesh.

They have a laugh and
Slap their knees
Because they couldn't care less
About the problems
That once consumed their days
When their hearts were put to their test.
They look back at themselves
Thinking about their wasted worries
When they approached life without light
In all of its flurried controversy.
Now six feet below the soil
They howl and joke about
Purely enjoying their time,
And you should too
Because we all end up
Just like the skeletons:
Simply dead and
Richly alive.

So many people fail to fully recognize
The beauty this world has to offer us.

Sometimes Beautiful Things Go Unnoticed

I sit under polka dotted skies
Waiting for the crickets to sing
To the beat in my fingertips.
That's the thing about crickets:
To most
They are simply noise
Whistling through the background,
An afterthought,
If they are even thought of at all.
Until suddenly
The silence takes over
Making the bugs' cries bold and apparent
In an unmistakable way.
Do you feel the disappointment?
The crickets incessantly scream but
Nobody cares to hear their orchestra
Until their lives prove dull.

She Cries

She cries at pots of boiling water
And at wolves that howl too loud at the moon.
She cries at her reflection in puddles.
She cries at the color purple.
She cries at plentiful, negligible strawberry seeds
And at faucets that drip for too long.
She cries at hourglasses
And at sand castles,
Sand castles being swept away
By the ocean's reckless hands.
She cries at tangled spider webs.
She cries at the clouds
Transitioning from white
To grey
To orange
To pink.
She cries at half bitten green tree leaves.
She cries at the wind licking her elbows,
And at snowflakes resting on a batted lash.
She cries and
She cries.
Its magnificence is all too massive so
She cries.
She cries.
She cries.

This world is splendid.

It's the people in it that are fucked up.

The Foundation of This Nation

Swollen eyes
And tired hearts
Lay in the hands of the aggressor.
America's white flag is bruised blue
From the abused.
America's white flag
Bleeds streaks of bright red tears.
America's white flag is stamped
With stars of subjection,
Victory stickers.

White Is Pure

White is pure
Probity
Rectitude
Ingrained in our brains
For years upon years
In our works of literature
In her dress
In the snowflakes
In new beginnings
Lies purity
In the color white
Lies hope
Innocence.
Black is polluted
Demonic
Corrupt
Ingrained in our brains
For decades upon decades
In our works of literature
In the dirt
In the night
In dark alleyways
Lies fear
In the color black
Lies danger

Sin.
I wonder who came up with that shit.
I bet he was white.

"Miserable America Assassinates My Character"

Colorblind

You mean to tell me
You don't see it?
You don't see
The chocolate in my pores,
The coil in my hair,
The limp in my stride,
The flare in my wear?
Don't turn a blind eye to
My best features.

Oh, honey
You can't notice
The gleam in my eyes,
The swell in my lips,
The hope in my heart,
The curve in my hips?
Don't claim unawareness.
Don't deny my story.

Don't tell me you can't hear
The strength in my voice,
The call of my prayers,
The pain in my history
For justice I blare!
Don't snub the struggle of my past

And present.

Recognize my agony.
Appreciate my beauty.
You don't see color?
Is that so?
My color is there!
The battle I feel.
I know you see it.
My pain is real!

They'll Mock Your Culture Because It's Not Theirs

My words are wrong.
I speak in the tongue of the uneducated.
"What?"
"What does *that* mean?"
Their lips are soaked with disdain.
They chuckle and chortle
Until their nostrils burn
From puffing out false laughter.
But one day
Years down the line
After forgetting the damage that was done
From saying, "I think you mean—"
They will be repeating my broken sentences.
They will snatch the words straight from my throat
Because now
Now it fits their culture.
Now it is slang,
Common and cool.
Now it is no longer
The words of the uneducated
Because now
Now it rolls of *their* tongue.
Now it is accepted
Now it is theirs

Because they stole it.
They steal everything
That was ever ours.

A Message to The Privileged: It's Always with Us

You see,
You're lucky.
You don't have to wake up with it every day.
It doesn't cross your mind in the middle
Of brushing your teeth.
It doesn't make your heart ache and burn
Similar to the sting that lingers in your chest
After a sharp cough.
It doesn't make your gut droop
With a cinder block so heavy
You can't eat.
You don't have to look at the news
And mourn over your
Brother
Sister
Mother
Cousin
Father
You didn't even know existed
Before that very moment when
The headlines crawled across the screen.
Because
You see,
For you,

That's the beauty of white privilege.
You don't have to carry it with you
If you don't want to.

Recognizing white privilege
Is not an attack on
Those with white skin.
It's shedding light on the system.
No one is blaming you
For being born into it.

They place boulders
On our backs and
Wait for us to break
But we are steel
So we never do.

Because I'm Black

"It's because you're black,"
She says.
Blatantly.
It came from the girl
With the pale white skin
And the freckles that roam
Across her face,
Traveling over the bridge
Of her nose.
And as the words escape her lips
There is a screaming, bubbling,
Howling, ferocious sensation
In my chest that burns
Like the taste of menthol.
My heart is filled
With nothing
But lava.
My eyes go black and red
With nothing
But the reflection of
Pitchforks in the foreground.
How dare she
How dare she
How dare she
How dare she

Repeats in my mind
A million times over.
A symphony of hatred,
Disgust.

I close my eyes and
Time travel to the sixties.
Quite frankly
I wouldn't be able to see the difference
Between now and then
And that is not
Because my eyes are closed,
It's because hers are.
Blind and bitter towards
Every ounce of my being,
Every drop of my success.
And why?
Because I'm black.

She can't fathom,
Not even a little bit,
That I,
A person of pigment
Overcame her,
One lack thereof.
What she doesn't realize is
How disparaging,
How disrespectful
That comment is because
Black is my identity,

Everything I am.
Black is beauty
Black is power
Black is resilience
Black is triumph
Black is struggle
Black is vigilance
Black is everything
That white girl can't bear to be.

But I won't stoop to her level.
I don't dare play the race card
And say she is
The way she is
Because she's white.
I won't say it.
Because it's not due
To the color of her skin,
But due to the hole in her heart.
A hole that could have been
Filled with
Kindness
Equality
Sanity
Justice
But that part of her is lost.
Or should I say gone?
Because I don't think
She ever intends on finding it,

If she even had it in the first place.

Now you tell me,
Is my creativity
Because I'm black?
Or what about
My positivity?
That surely must be
Because I'm black right?
Especially in
White privileged America
Where it is just so easy
For a black girl to keep
A smile on her face through
All of this overwhelming "equality."
Or my charisma
My awards
My trophies
My GPA
My athleticism
My intelligence
All of it
Because I'm black?
Not because I am accomplished
Not because I am worthy
Not because I deserve it
Not because I work hard
Not because I bust my ass
Day after day

To get to where I am
But why?
Because I'm black.

None of it adds up.
I'm doing the digits,
Carrying the one,
Using a calculator
But still
Still
I can't seem to discover
Why there is so much
Ignorance
Animosity
Aggression.
I guess it's too abstruse of a concept,
Something I can't
Wrap my head around.
That must be
Because I'm black.

(The poem that started it all)

She shoved something sour in my mouth
And I was forced to swallow it.

It left me with a stomach ache
For days.

When the Going Gets Tough

They'll throw rocks at the nape of your neck,
Stab you with a skewer and roast you
With an apple in your mouth.
They'll tear your skin open with butter knives,
Wring your spine with their bare hands,
Steal your clothes while you're in the shower;
You'll be naked and vulnerable.
They'll plunge a finger in your open wound
Because they can,
Yell obscenities in your face until
Their stale breath makes your bones quiver.
They'll label you;
They'll stamp a number on your forehead and
Slap a barcode on your wrist.
They'll shove you to the ground and
Trample you with their boot soles.
But, child, they are small
And you shall overcome
Because that
That is what it takes
In order to be great.

How do people have so much
space in their heart for hate?
Because nothing else is filling it.

Be a Smart Bee

>
>I am a bee
>I sit on flower beds
>And spin honey
>But don't be fooled
>I'm striped with yellow caution signs
>Because if you swat
>I will sting.

* * *

I am a smart bee
And when you swat
It takes everything in my being
Not to sting back.
If I partake in your dirty games
And pierce you with my spear
I will be satisfied
But in due time
My tail will fall,
I will die,
And you will have the last laugh.

So
I will buzz on
To sit on flower beds and
Spin honey.

People can be cruel
But you shall continue
To create sweetness for
Juice is only extracted
From the ripest fruit
When it is squeezed.

I wish society was like a garden
With all of its different kinds
Sprouting beautifully calm.
Individually and together.

Above all
Love is the answer

Epilogue

The Strength in Altruism

I find it endlessly beautiful how a single candle has the ability to spread its light on to a million other wicks without losing its own flame. That is what I strive to be. I am fully aware of how easy it is for a person to have their internal light dimmed in a world of injustice, depression and anxiety. This is why I am inclined to permeate radiance to those who have lost all hope in humanity. I want to saturate this earth in positivity and I strive to spread joy in every way I can, which is why I brought my love for writing, my appetite for art and my passion for helping others to create this book. This is the template for me to write down my battles along with my victories, and through all of this it is important to note that there is still incentive to be cheerful. I want people to understand that even in a world of pain and suffering there are still hundreds upon thousands of reasons to be happy. Even in the darkest of times, people should have a motive to wake up every morning with a smile on their face, realizing it is simply a blessing to have a heart that is still beating.

Everybody has a burden. Everybody is fighting a battle that is undetectable at face value. People have pains so deep and skeletons so closeted that it is simply impossible to see with the naked eye. That is why it is so incredibly important that people are kind to one another because nobody truly knows what demons a person is fighting. I wrote some of mine down, bound them to a spine, added a cover and called it a book but you don't have to create a collection of poetry for me to know that you are fighting your own demons as well. Ultimately, I want you to know that whatever you are going through, everything will be better in the end; if it is not better than it is simply not the end. So keep smiling. Keep trudging on because happiness is attainable if you focus on what is good in the world and you continue to spread kindness.

    Primarily, altruism is not about giving something of yours away, it is about spreading what you have to others without losing it yourself. I have an internal flame so bright it is untamable and I spread it onto everything that I touch. I am a candle and that is why I am altruistic.

    Finally, if you have gained anything after concluding this book, I hope you have gained the knowledge that there is strength in altruism, there is potential in positivity, and ultimately there is power in words.

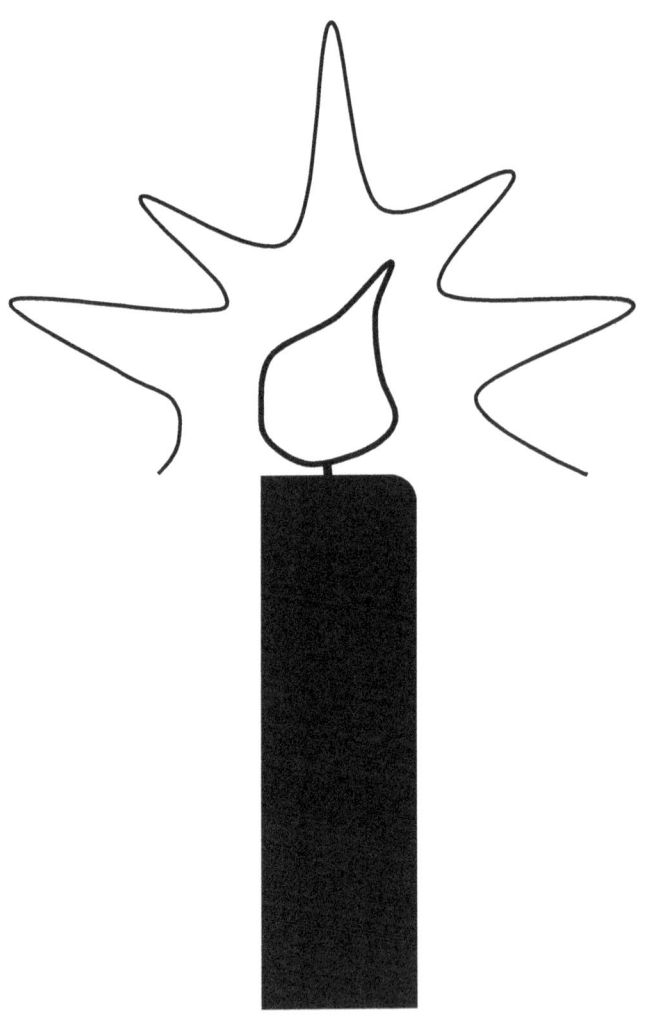

About the Author

Hilary Besson is a writer and artist, who is currently an eighteen-year-old freshmen at the University of Massachusetts Amherst. She has no formal training in either subject, but casually writes and creates art whenever she feels inspired. She has always had a knack for writing, but she began writing poetry recreationally in the spring of 2016, her senior year of high school. The summer of that year is when she decided she wanted to publish her work in the hopes that her writing will inspire people and free them from the weight of their burdens as much as it has freed her.

For more information or to view her artwork visit
www.hilarybesson.com

REFLECT:

www.ingramcontent.com/pod-product-compliance
Lightning Source LLC
LaVergne TN
LVHW041253080426
835510LV00009B/711